★SUPERSTAR★ QUARTERBACKS

RICHARD J. BRENNER

EAST END PUBLISHING, LTD.
Huntington, New York

AUTHOR'S NOTE: The players in this book are all gifted athletes, but they all had to work hard to achieve their dreams. And the work never stops.

"Winning the Super Bowl is the ultimate goal for an NFL player, but I'm not going to spend the rest of my career on cruise-control," said Peyton Manning. "I'm going to work as hard as I ever have to get better and try to win it again."

You can become a superstar, also, if *you're* willing to work as hard to achieve *your goals* and *express your special talents* as Peyton Manning is to achieve *his*. And there are lots of areas for you to consider besides athletics. You might want to become an artist or musician or writer, or you might decide to work for world peace. You can accomplish whatever you put your mind to, as long as you *set your goals* and *work hard to reach them.*

This book is also dedicated, as all my books are, to the children of the world. I wish that all of you could live in peaceful, loving surroundings, free from fear and bigotry of every type.

I also want to express great appreciation to everybody whose time and talents have contributed to this book, including John Douglas, Janie DeVos, Jim Wasserman, Jamie Calsyn, Rob Trignali and Ellen Raimondo Shupp.

I also want to express sincere thanks to Janet Speakman, Ed Masessa and Carolyn Longest.

Copy Editor: **John Douglas**
Research Editor: **Janie DeVos**
Book Design: **Studio 31, Inc.**

Photo Credits: SportsChrome supplied the following images, with the photographers' names in parenthesis: Peyton Manning: P. 6 (**Tom DiPace**); the cover image of Eli Manning and the image on P. 9 (**Bryan Yablonsky**); Philip Rivers: P. 22 (**Michael Zito**); the cover image of Drew Brees and P. 27 and P. 30 (**Rob Tringali**). The remaining images were supplied by Icon SMI, as per the following: Peyton Manning: The cover image as well as the ones on P. 3 (**Joe Robbins**) and 4 (**Mark Cowan**); Eli Manning: P. 10 (**Daniel Gluskoter**) and 12 (**Albert Dickson**); Vince Young: The cover image and P. 13 and 16 (**Ed Wolfstein**); P. 14 (**Wade Payne**); Philip Rivers: the cover image and P. 19 (**Matt A. Brown**); P. 20 (**Sean Meyers**); Tony Romo: the cover image and P. 23 and 26 (**James D. Smith**), P. 24 (**Karl Wright**); Drew Brees: P. 28 (**Richard Brightly**).

ISBN: 0-943403-73-1   ISBN-13: 978-0-943403-73-1

Published by **EAST END PUBLISHING, LTD.**
112 Abbott Dr.
Huntington, NY 11743
Printed in the United States of America by Banta Book Group.

Richard J. Brenner, America's best-selling sportswriter, has written more than 70 exciting sports titles. For details on how to order some of them, see back page of this book.

* * *

Mr. Brenner is also available to speak at schools. For details, including fees, you may e-mail him directly at: rjbrenner1@gmail.com, or write to him c/o EEP, 112 Abbott Drive Huntington, NY 11743.

PEYTON MANNING

Born: March 24, 1976, in New Orleans, Louisiana
Height: 6-5   Weight: 230
College: Tennessee   Round drafted: First   NFL Seasons: 9

CAREER STATS

Att.	Comp.	Pct.	Yards	TD	Int.	QB Rating
4,890	3,131	64.0	37,586	275	139	94.4

During his nine seasons in the NFL, Peyton Manning had set scores of passing records, won a pair of MVP Awards, and helped the Indianapolis Colts become one of the elite teams in the league. But many critics claimed that Manning would have to win some big games, especially a Super Bowl, before he could be considered a truly great quarterback.

"Fair or not, Super Bowls are how you judge quarterbacks," said Tennessee Titans' defensive coordinator Jim Schwartz. "Peyton has done everything else. He's been the MVP, and he'll probably own every passing record worth owning by the time he retires. There's only one thing left for him to do."

It was true that the Manning-led Colts did not have a great, or even a winning, record in their six playoff appearances prior to the 2006 season. But even after he'd led the Colts to a dramatic, comeback win against the New England Patriots in the 2006 AFC Championship Game, a win that put them into the Super Bowl for the first time in his career, many people still thought that Manning had to win on the biggest stage to validate his greatness.

"It's not just about getting to the Super Bowl," said football analyst John Madden, who had coached the Oakland Raiders to victory in Super Bowl XI. "Peyton has to win it to erase that, 'Yes, but,' that you constantly hear about him. Then, they'll never be able to say it again.

"He deserves it, because he works so hard at perfecting his game," continued Madden, after he had watched Manning lead the Colts back from an 18-point deficit, the biggest comeback ever in a conference championship game. "Even though he was blessed with tremendous ability, he's always worked to get better. I don't know if there's ever been a player who has practiced as hard and watched as much film as Peyton has."

Although Manning had heard all the talk about his failure to lead the Colts to the Super Bowl in previous seasons, he refused to put that monkey on his back.

"I've always looked at it as we win and lose as a team," he explained. "I've never shied away from taking responsibility for my play, but all those times that we lost in the playoffs, I just don't think our team was good enough. Other people have other explanations, but that's how I look at it."

While Manning seemed to take his critics in stride, Tony Dungy, the Colts' mild-mannered coach, reacted sharply to the idea that Manning was somehow a failure.

"I guess they won't shut up until we've won it," said Dungy. "But Peyton Manning is a great quarterback, and anybody who doesn't know that, doesn't know much about football."

Then, Manning went out and put an end to all the talk by leading the Colts to a 29-17 win over the Chicago Bears in Super Bowl XLI, and winning the game's MVP trophy.

"Peyton is a tremendous player, a great leader," said Dungy, who became the first African-American head coach to win a Super Bowl. "He prepares. He works. He does everything he can to win games. People think he had to win a Super Bowl to validate his career, but I never agreed with that line of thinking. But there's nothing that anybody can say now. He's a Super Bowl champion, a future Hall of Famer, and one of the greatest ever to play the game."

Most people would find it hard to grow up in the shadow of a legend, but Eli Manning had to find growing room while sharing a house with two of them.

His father, Archie, had been a college All-American and then a Pro Bowl quarterback, before he became a broadcaster for the New Orleans Saints, as well as one of the most respected people in the Crescent City.

As if that wasn't a high enough hurdle to clear, an older brother, Peyton, had been named the 1993 Gatorade National High School Player of the Year, before going on to become an All-American college quarterback at the University of Tennessee, and then a perennial All-Pro pick in the NFL.

Eli, who is five years younger than Peyton, still speaks about the thrill of finally beating his brother in a backyard basketball game when Eli was 17 years old.

"I destroyed him," said Eli, while smiling at the memory.

ELI MANNING

Born: January 3, 1981, in New Orleans, Louisiana
Height: 6-4   Weight: 225
College: Mississippi   Round drafted: First   NFL Seasons: 3

CAREER STATS

Att.	Comp.	Pct.	Yards	TD	Int.	QB Rating
1,276	690	54.1	8,049	54	44	73.2

"That was the first thing I ever beat him in, besides ping-pong and pool. Getting that first win was a big step for me."

Eli carved out an excellent high school career at Newman, the same school that Peyton had starred at, and was named the 1998 *USA Today* Player of the Year in Louisiana. But at his first practice at the University of Mississippi—where the trophy case is filled with mementos of his father's accomplishments—Manning had been uncertain about his ability to succeed, and anxious about being accepted by his teammates.

"I was nervous, because I didn't know if I could even complete a pass at the college level," recalled Eli. "Forget about trying to be like Peyton. I was also worried that

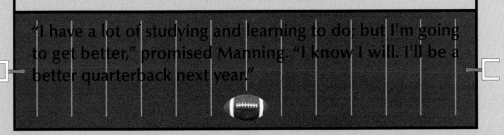

my teammates would think that the only reason I was even there was because I had a brother who could play."

It wasn't until right before his third year, his first as a starter, that Manning declared that he was ready to step out from the shadows of his father and brother.

"I'm not worried about living up to what my dad did or about being as good as my brother," said Eli, who completed 18 straight passes and threw for five touchdowns in his first start for the Rebels. "All I'm thinking about is being the best player I can be."

Manning did so well during his college career that he set or tied 47 of the Rebels' single-game, season, and career passing records, most of which had been set by his father. The Chargers made Manning the first pick of the 2004 draft, but since he didn't want to play for San Diego, they made a draft day deal with the New York Giants that netted them Philip Rivers.

"Eli is a once-in-a-decade player," said Ernie Accorsi, who was the Giants' general manager. "He's the type of quarterback you wait a long time for."

Manning took over as Big Blue's starter right after the mid-point of his rookie season, and has gone on to help lead the Giants into the playoffs in each of the past two seasons. And while he hasn't progressed as quickly as some people hoped, the Giants still feel that he's the one to lead them to a championship.

"He is definitely the guy to lead us where we want to go," said team president John Mara. "We know he has the talent and the work ethic to rise to the next level, just like his brother has."

VINCE YOUNG

Born: May 18, 1983, in Houston, Texas
Height: 6-5   Weight: 233
College: Texas   Round drafted: First   NFL Seasons: 1

CAREER STATS

Att.	Comp.	Pct.	Yards	TD	Int.	QB Rating
357	184	51.5	2,199	12	13	66.7

Vince Young grew up in a tough section of Houston, where crime and drugs are as unsparing as the summer heat, and lives get wasted far too often. Young didn't have to look very far to find bad examples to follow. His father was a criminal, who was in and out of jail during most of Young's childhood. While his mother, who was addicted to drugs when Young was growing up, couldn't even take care of herself, let alone her son. After he'd taken a few minor missteps of his own, Young quickly decided that he wasn't going to throw his life into a waste bin.

"The guys I rolled with were gang members," said Young. "Some got shot. Some went to jail. I could have been in the same situation. I had to learn right from wrong. If I hadn't, I wouldn't be where I am today."

Young began to channel his energy into sports, and became a four-sport star at Madison High School, in Houston, Texas. In his senior season on the gridiron, Young totaled 3,819 yards and 59 touchdowns passing and running, and was named the 2001 Texas 5-A Offensive High School Player of the Year.

"He's as fast and as elusive as Michael Vick, but he's a better overall passer," said Madison coach Roy Seals, comparing Young to the Atlanta Falcons' quarterback. "In fact, there isn't anything he can't do on a football field."

Young's outstanding play won him a scholarship to the University of Texas, but the coaching staff didn't like his three-quarter throwing motion, and thought about turning him into a wide receiver. Young, however, met with the coaches and asked them to give him a chance to stay at quarterback.

"There are lots of guys who have terrible throwing motions—much worse than mine," said Young. "But they still get the ball downfield, and that's all that matters."

Young developed dramatically during his three years as the Longhorns' starting quarterback, and got the ball downfield so well in 2005, his final season with Texas, that he amassed 4,086 yards passing and running, which shattered the school's single-season record by nearly 1,000 yards. Young, who won the Maxwell Award as the top player in college football, capped off his collegiate career by leading Texas to their first national title in 35 years, when he engineered a last-second 41-38 upset of USC in the 2006 Rose Bowl.

"That was one of the greatest performances in college football history," said Texas coach Mack Brown, after he'd watched Young tally two touchdowns in the game's waning minutes. "The bigger the challenge, the better he plays."

The Tennessee Titans had also seen what Young could do, and selected him with the third pick of the 2006 NFL draft. He was supposed to sit and learn the offense, but he took over as the starter in the team's fourth game, and quickly showed the same dazzling skills that he had shown in Texas. In his 13 games as the starter, Young led the team to four fourth-quarter comeback wins, while passing for 12 touchdowns and running for seven.

His spectacular play earned him the NFL Offensive Rookie of the Year award, as well as a spot in the Pro Bowl, after Philip Rivers was sidelined with an injury.

"Playing in the Pro Bowl was a dream come true," said Young. "I've come a long way, and I still have a lot to learn, but I'm going to keep working and getting better."

Rivers has worn No. 17 since he was in ninth grade, an expression of affection for his father, who wore that number when he played high school football.

Philip Rivers was introduced to football by his father Steve, a long-time high school coach in Alabama. From the time he was five years old, Rivers was on the practice field, handing out water to the players, and soaking up all the knowledge that he could. Afterwards, he would go home and work on the plays he had learned that day. By the time he was 10 years old, he had the team's offense down pat, and knew that he wanted to be an NFL quarterback.

"Some of my fondest memories about Philip are from when he was a ball boy," recalled his dad. "He had so much fun, and I loved having him with me."

Rivers went on to play for three years at Athens High School, where he was the starting quarterback for his final two seasons with the Golden Eagles, and also played safety on defense.

"He really didn't have the speed that most defensive backs have," said Allen Creasy, who was an assistant coach.

"He'd mastered the offense by the time he was 10 years old," said Allen Creasy. "I'm a coach's son, too, but I didn't have his knowledge when I was 10."

PHILIP RIVERS

Born: December 8, 1981, in Decatur, Alabama
Height: 6-5   Weight: 228
College: N. C. State   Round drafted: First   NFL Seasons: 3

CAREER STATS

Att.	Comp.	Pct.	Yards	TD	Int.	QB Rating
490	301	61.4	3,536	23	10	90.5

"But he had such a good understanding and feel for the game that he wound up making 10 interceptions in his senior season."

Rivers then went to North Carolina State, but didn't think he'd make it through his first college practice.

"As I dropped back to try my first pass, I thought to myself, 'I will never complete a pass,'" recalled Rivers. "The players were so much faster than the ones I had played against in high school, and I didn't know if I'd be able to keep up."

Despite his initial fear, Rivers went on to become a four-year starter for the Wolfpack, and threw for 13,484 passing yards, the second-most in NCAA history.

"Philip is a *wow* guy, and there's only a few of them,"

> "The guy is a born leader," said Antonio Gates, the Bolts' All-Pro tight end. "Watch how he interacts with everybody. I've never seen anything like it."

said Mike Barry, an assistant coach at N.C. State. "There are a whole bunch of what I would call *nice* players, but Philip is a *wow*."

Rivers had also impressed A.J. Smith, the general manager of the Chargers, who pulled off a deal at the 2004 draft that brought the young quarterback to San Diego. During his first two seasons with the Bolts, however, Rivers played behind Drew Brees, and he spent so little time on the field that he wound up throwing a total of only 30 passes. Although he practiced hard, and studied film late into the night, the lack of game-time action was hard for him to deal with.

"Sundays were tough," admitted Rivers, who had been a starting quarterback for six straight seasons, starting with his junior year in high school. "I look back on those two years, and a lot of things weren't fun. But Sundays were worse than the other days."

> "I'm going to get my shot at some point," said Rivers. "Whenever it is, wherever it is, I'll be a starter on some team. That's what drives me."

After the 2005 season, Brees signed with the New Orleans Saints, however, and Rivers was ready to grab the reins.

"I'm excited to get out there and show what I can do," said Rivers. "But, more importantly, what this team can do with me at quarterback."

Rivers didn't waste any time in showing what he could do by earning a ticket to the Pro Bowl, and leading the Bolts to a 14-2 mark, the best record in the NFL in 2006. According to Norv Turner, who was hired as the head coach for the 2007 season, the future looks even brighter.

"Rivers has played only one season," explained Turner. "He's nowhere near the quarterback he is going to be in three or four years."

TONY ROMO

Born: April 21, 1980, in San Diego, California
Height: 6-2   Weight: 225
College: E. Illinois   Round drafted: N/A   NFL Seasons: 4

CAREER STATS

Att.	Comp.	Pct.	Yards	TD	Int.	QB Rating
337	220	65.3	2,903	19	13	95.1

Tony Romo didn't come into the league from a top-notch college football program, or as a high-level draft pick. Romo, in fact, was passed over in the 2003 draft, and signed with the Dallas Cowboys as a free agent, after hundreds of higher-rated players had been picked. But he didn't allow his being overlooked in the draft to dampen his confidence.

"In life, you can get where you are from different directions," explained Romo. "It's what you do when you get there that counts."

Big-time college football schools had also bypassed him after he'd graduated from Burlington (Wis.) High School. The only school to offer him a scholarship was Eastern Illinois, which has a relatively small-time football program. And even then, the Panthers' head coach,

Bob Spoo, had to be sold on Romo by an assistant coach, Steve Garber.

"We hadn't even bothered to watch him play football, but Steve had seen him play for the Burlington basketball team," recalled Spoo. "He convinced me that Tony had great leadership qualities and the ability to make plays. In any sport, that's what you look for, a leader and playmaker."

Romo struggled at first, and even thought about quitting the team in his first season. But he made tremendous strides the following year by working on his weak points.

"He was a gym rat," said Spoo. "He would stay afterwards and practice throws he wasn't happy with. He's not afraid to work."

All that effort paid off in a big way for Romo, who set the school and conference record for career touchdown tosses, with 85, and who, in his senior season, snared the 2002 Walter Payton Award, which is given to the best player in Division 1-AA.

Despite his accomplishments, however, all 32 NFL teams still passed him over in the draft and, in spite of all his hard work, Romo still spent more than three seasons as a backup quarterback. It wasn't until the seventh game of the 2006 season that Cowboys' coach Bill Parcells entrusted Romo with his first NFL start.

Romo responded to the challenge by leading Dallas to five wins in his first starts, which included a team record-tying five touchdown passes against the Tampa Bay Buccaneers. Romo cooled off a bit afterwards, but he still did enough to earn Pro Bowl honors, and help lead the Cowboys into the playoffs.

"At each level, I've had to figure out what I had to do to be successful," said Romo. "It takes me a little time, but I get there."

DREW BREES

Born: January 15, 1979, in Austin, Texas
Height: 6-0   Weight: 209
College: Purdue   Round drafted: Second   NFL Seasons: 6

CAREER STATS

Att.	Comp.	Pct.	Yards	TD	Int.	QB Rating
2,363	1,481	62.7	16,766	106	64	87.5

Although Drew Brees has sometimes been underestimated because he isn't tall and doesn't have a powerful arm, he has usually found a way to come out on top.

"I've seen plenty of big, fast, tall guys that can't play a lick," noted Brees. "And I've seen plenty of guys who don't look the part, but they've just got what it takes. They have a certain drive in them that you can't measure in a 40-yard dash time or a distance throw. But at the end of a game or the end of a season, they're on the winning side. It's not about size or numbers, it's about winning."

Brees showed that he knew how to win during his time at Westlake High School, in Austin, Texas, where he played for four years and never lost a single game. In his senior season, he led the Chaparrals to a 16-0 record and the 1996 State Class 5A title, while setting the school record for single-season and career touchdown passes.

"He always had that knack of getting the ball to a receiver, and getting us into the end zone," said Westlake coach Derek Long. "I still see that ability when I watch him today."

Despite his unbeaten record, many college programs, including the University of Texas, didn't think that Brees had what it takes to become a big-time college quarterback. So, he went up north to Purdue, and went on to set most of the Big Ten Conference career records for passing, including touchdown passes and yards gained.

In 2000, his senior season, Brees won the Maxwell Trophy as the best player in college football, and then led the Boilermakers to the 2001 Rose Bowl, their first appearance in the big game since 1967. Brees, who was also a superior

student, won the Socrates Award for outstanding athletic and academic achievements and for his dedication to community service.

"Drew was probably the best quarterback ever to play at Purdue, and he was a credit to the university," said Boilermaker coach Joe Tiller. "He was a winner on the field and off of it."

Although many NFL scouts were concerned that he wasn't tall enough to see over defensive linemen, the San Diego Chargers took a chance on Brees in the second round of the 2001 draft. During his first three years with the Bolts, Brees struggled more than he succeeded, winning and losing the starting job more than once. But Brees blossomed during the 2004 season, and was chosen for the Pro Bowl after leading the Chargers to their first playoff appearance in a decade.

But, after another Pro Bowl season in 2005, he signed with the New Orleans Saints. He was coming to a franchise with a long history of losing, and to a city still suffering from the devastating effects of Hurricane Katrina, which had nearly washed it away the year before.

"I know this town is craving a winner," said Brees, at his first press conference in New Orleans, "and you're going to get one."

At the time, Brees' bravado seemed like so much hot air, but then he went out and delivered on his promise by leading the Saints to a division title and only the second playoff win in their 40-year history.

"Winning isn't an accident for him," said Saints' head coach Sean Payton. "He's been a winner at every level he's ever played at."

"Without Drew Brees, they would have finished 6-10, instead of 10-6," said former Saints' quarterback Bobby Hebert. "That's how much I think he meant to this team."

ORDER FORM

If you enjoyed this book, you might want to order some of the other exciting titles written by Richard J. Brenner, the best-selling sportswriter in America.

QTY

BASEBALL SUPERSTARS ALBUM 2007: Includes 16 full-sized, full-color photos of 16 of the game's top players—including Derek Jeter, Albert Pujols, Ryan Howard, and Justin Morneau—plus biographical sketches and career stats.
48 pages, 8-1/2 x 11. $6.99 US.   _____

SUPERSTAR QUARTERBACKS: Includes biographical sketches and 18 full-color photos of six top quarterbacks: Peyton Manning, Eli Manning, Vince Young, Philip Rivers, Tony Romo and Drew Brees. 32 pages, 6 x 9. $3.99 US.   _____

TOM BRADY * LADAINIAN TOMLINSON: A dual-biography of two of the NFL's top players. The book includes 16 action-packed color photos.
144 pages, 5 x 8. $5.99 US.   _____

EXTREME ACTION STARS: Includes 15 action-packed photos and biographical sketches of Shaun White, Danny Way, Travis Pastrana, Bucky Lasek, and Blair Morgan. 32 pages, 8-1/2 x 11. $4.99 US.   _____

BRETT FAVRE: An easy-to-read photo-filled biography of one of football's all-time greats. Written especially for younger children. 32 pages, 8 x 8. $4.50 US.   _____

SPECIAL OFFER: The books listed below are being offered for $1.00 each, plus normal shipping charges.

MARK McGWIRE: An easy-to-read photo-filled biography of one of baseball's all-time greats. Written especially for younger children. 32 pages, 8 x 8. Originally published at $4.50 US.   _____

FOOTBALL'S SUPERSTAR ALBUM 2000: Includes 16 full-sized, full-color photos of 16 of the game's top players, plus biographical sketches and career stats. 48 pages, 8-1/2 x 11. Originally published at $4.99 US.   _____

Total Number of Book(s) Ordered   _____

Add $1.50 per book if you want book(s) autographed by author.   _____

Total Cost of Books   _____

TAX (NY State residents must add appropriate sales tax)   _____

Shipping Charges (in the US) $1.95 per book, up to a maximum of $9.75 on orders of 10 or fewer books.   _____

TOTAL PAYMENT ENCLOSED: (All payments must be in US currency; checks and money orders only; credit cards not accepted).   _____

(Please print clearly.)

NAME _____

ADDRESS _____

CITY _____ STATE _____ ZIP CODE _____

SEND PAYMENTS TO: **EAST END PUBLISHING, LTD.**
                     112 Abbott Drive, Huntington, NY 11743.

Discounts are available on orders of 25 or more books.
For details write or email: rjbrenner1@gmail.com
Terms are subject to change without notice.